1 Introduction

The U.S. labor market is large and multifaceted. Often-cited indicators, such as the unemployment rate or payroll employment, each measure a specific dimension of labor market activity, and it is not uncommon for different indicators to send conflicting signals about labor market conditions, especially at monthly frequencies. Even the most prominent indicators can disagree. To cite one instance, the Bureau of Labor Statistics (BLS)'s employment report for December 2013 indicated that the unemployment rate had fallen 0.3 percentage point while payroll employment rose only 74,000. Thus, the unemployment rate was signalling a strong improvement in the labor market and payroll employment a tepid (at best) improvement.

In such situations, analysts naturally look at additional indicators to try to infer the true rate of change in labor market conditions. But the desire to use more information is not limited to occasional situations. In recent years, for example, some observers have emphasized labor force participation and involuntary part-term employment as additional dimensions that merit particular attention, suggesting that these measures point to a more slowly improving labor market than does the more prominent unemployment rate. However, it is often difficult to know how to weigh the signals from various indicators, especially when those indicators are as diverse as, say, wage rates and consumer sentiment. A statistical model, while no substitute for judicious consideration, can be useful because it provides one relatively non-judgemental way to summarize information from numerous indicators.

There have been several efforts along these lines in recent years. For example, Barnes et al. (2007), Hakkio and Willis (2013) and Zmitrowicz and Khan (2014) developed principal component models of 12, 24, and 8 labor market indicators, respectively. Principal component models attempt to summarize the common movement in a number of data series. For the broader economy, the Chicago Fed National Activity Index is derived from a principal component analysis of 85 monthly indicators (including 24 indicators from the labor market).[1] In a related vein, numerous researchers have developed factor models for now-casting and forecasting aggregate output from a large number of macroeconomic indicators (for example, Stock and Watson, 2002; Giannone, Reichlin and Small, 2008; Stock and Watson, 2011).

This paper describes a dynamic factor model of nineteen labor market indicators and the resulting labor market conditions index (LMCI). Section 2 describes the indicators that we include in the model. Section 3 describes the factor model in some detail, including our detrending procedure, and how each indicator relates to the estimated LMCI. In section 4, we explain why we believe the LMCI is best viewed as an indicator of changes in labor market conditions and that its level is not a measure of the magnitude of labor market slack. Section 5 describes the behavior of the LMCI broadly over history and highlights movements in the LMCI since the be-

---

1. http://www.chicagofed.org/publications/cfnai/index

ginning of the Great Recession. In section 6, we use the model to argue that the decline in the unemployment rate has somewhat overstated the improvement in labor market conditions in recent years. Section 7 provides concluding remarks.

2 Labor Market Indicators

Information about the state of the labor market is available monthly from a variety of sources, including official government statistics, privately gathered data, and surveys of businesses and households. We include in our model a large, but certainly not exhaustive, set of the available data—19 indicators in all.

Because a model of this type emphasizes the common movements among indicators, it can be sensitive to the balance across different types of indicators included. It is therefore desirable to avoid weighting the scale too heavily with indicators that reflect closely related aspects of the labor market. That is to say, more indicators is not always better. On the one hand, including two measures of a similar object likely enhances the model's ability to identify signal (common movement) from noise (idiosyncratic variation). On the other hand, including too many measures of the same thing may distort the picture in their favor. For example, if, in addition to the official unemployment rate (designated "U-3" by the BLS), we also included the U-1, U-2, U-4, and U-5 underutilization rates—which are highly correlated with U-3—we would bias the LMCI to look more like the unemployment rate.

With this consideration in mind, we chose indicators covering the broad categories of unemployment and underemployment, employment, workweeks, wages, vacancies, hiring, layoffs, quits, and surveys of consumers' and businesses' perceptions. Table 1 lists the indicators and provides some information about the form, source, and availability of each measure; they are discussed in more detail below. In order to enhance the real-time usefulness of our index, all data are measured at a monthly frequency and seasonally adjusted. Accordingly, the resulting LMCI does not exhibit seasonal variation.

We begin our estimation sample with July 1976 because that is when most published series calculated from the CPS begin. However, as noted in Table 1, some indicators are not available as far back as 1976. Perhaps more importantly, the most recent month available for a few of the indicators routinely lags the others by one or two months. In particular, the most-recent observations for the hiring and quit rates from the Job Openings and Labor Turnover Survey (JOLTS) always lag the Current Population Survey (CPS) or Current Employment Statistics (CES) data by at least one month—and often two months. The indicators from the National Federation of Independent Businesses (NFIB)'s Small Business Employment Trends, net hiring plans and unfilled job openings, are occasionally missing for the most-recent month, particularly when the Employment Situation is released early in the month. In either case, dynamic factor models are

Table 1. Labor Market Indicators Included in the LMCI

Indicator	Units	Source	Begins
Unemployment and underemployment			
Unemployment rate	Percent of labor force	CPS	1976m7
Labor force participation rate	Percent of population	CPS	1976m7
Involuntary part-time employment	Percent of employment	CPS	1976m7
Employment			
Private employment	Percent of population	CES	1976m7
Government employment	Percent of population	CES	1976m7
Temporary help services employment	Percent of population	CES	1982m1
Workweeks			
Average weekly hours of production workers	Hours per week	CES	1976m7
Average weekly hours of persons at work	Hours per week	CPS	1976m7
Wages			
Average hourly earnings of production workers	Dollars per hour, percent change from previous year	CES	1976m7
Vacancies			
Composite help-wanted index	Index	CB	1976m7
Hiring			
Hiring rate[†]	Percent of nonfarm employment	JOLTS	1990m4
Transition rate from unemployment to employment	Percent of unemployed in previous month	CPS	1976m7
Layoffs			
Insured unemployment rate	Percent of covered employment	ETA	1976m7
Job losers unemployed less than five weeks	Percent of employed in previous month	CPS	1976m7
Quits			
Quit rate[†]	Percent of nonfarm employment	JOLTS	1990m4
Job leavers unemployed less than five weeks	Percent of employed in previous month	CPS	1976m7
Surveys of consumers' and businesses' perceptions			
Job availability	Percent of respondents answering that jobs are plentiful minus percent answering that jobs are hard to get	CB	1978m1
Net hiring plans[*]	Percent of firms planning to expand employment in the next 3 months minus percent of firms planning to cut jobs	NFIB	1986m1
Unfilled jobs openings[*]	Percent of firms with a job opening they could not fill	NFIB	1986m1

Notes: CB = Conference Board and Barnichon (2010); CES = Bureau of Labor Statistics, Current Employment Statistics; CPS = Bureau of Labor Statistics, Current Population Survey; ETA = Department of Labor, Employment and Training Administration; JOLTS = Bureau of Labor Statistics, Job Openings and Labor Turnover Survey; NFIB = National Federation of Independent Business. See the appendix for additional details. Availability lags (†) or may lag (*) that of the CES/CPS data.

well-suited to deal with unbalanced panels like this one.

The remainder of this section briefly describes the indicators included in the model. Details about their construction and about the underlying source data can be found in the appendix.

2.1 Unemployment and Underemployment

The *unemployment rate*, plotted in Figure 1a, is one of the most closely watched labor market indicators. It measures the number of persons who do not currently have a job and that are available for work and have been actively searching for a job within the prior 4 weeks, and is thus arguably the most direct measure of the underutilization of labor resources. Movements in unemployment tend to be closely related to movements in aggregate economic activity. (The red line in this and subsequent figures is the estimated trend, which is explained in section 3.)

The *labor force participation rate (LFPR)*, the number of persons either working or looking for work as a percentage of the population, also provides a measure of labor market utilization. It is plotted in Figure 1b. Although the unemployment rate provides the most direct measure of underutilization, the LFPR does respond to labor market conditions. For example, in tight labor markets, persons previously not in the labor force may enter because job opportunities are plentiful; in contrast, in slack labor markets, individuals may leave or not enter the labor force because job prospects are dim.

As many observers have noted, there are prominent trends in the labor force participation rate reflecting structural influences such as the aging of the baby boom generation, increasing longevity, and higher levels of education.[2] Thus, distinguishing cyclical movements in the LFPR from trend is particularly important.

A third measure of underutilization we include in the LMCI is *involuntary part-time employment* (Figure 1c), specifically the number of persons working part-time for economic reasons. Although these persons have jobs, they are working fewer than 35 hours per week for reasons such as slack work, unfavorable business conditions, inability to find full-time work, or seasonal declines in demand. Including this indicator captures a degree of underutilization that would not be measured by the unemployment rate or the LFPR.[3]

2.2 Employment

The number of persons employed is another obviously important indicator of labor market conditions. We use nonfarm payroll employment from the CES, rather than employment from the

---

2. See Aaronson et al. (2014) for a discussion of recent developments and future prospects.

3. We would have liked to include a measure of persons marginally attached to the labor force (from the CPS). In some respects, we think this indicator could be superior to the LFPR as a measure of underutilization, because such persons seem most likely to join or remain out of the labor force in response to labor market conditions. Alas, because the series is available only starting in 1994, it proved difficult to detrend and difficult for the factor model to infer its cyclical dynamics.

Figure 1. Underemployment Indicators

(a) Unemployment Rate

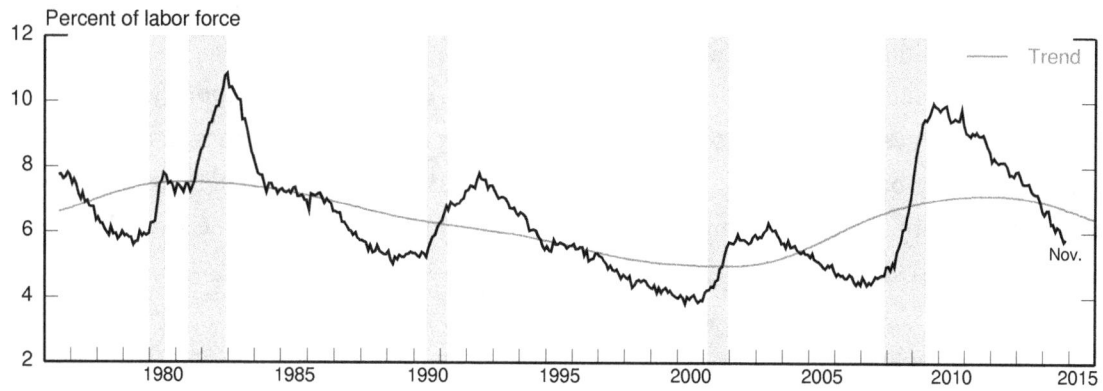

Source: Current Population Survey.
Note: Gray shaded bands indicate a period of business recession as defined by the NBER.

(b) Labor Force Participation Rate

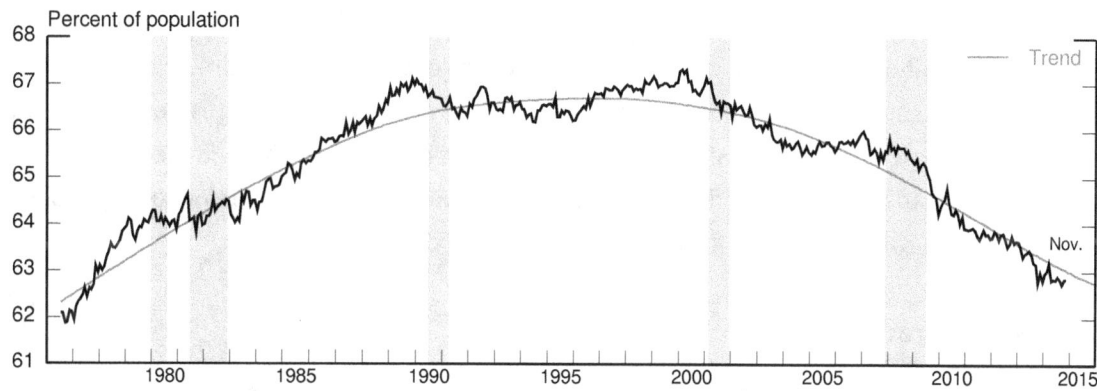

Source: Current Population Survey.
Note: Adjusted to account for changes in population weights. Gray shaded bands indicate a period of business recession as defined by the NBER.

(c) Involuntary Part-Time Employment

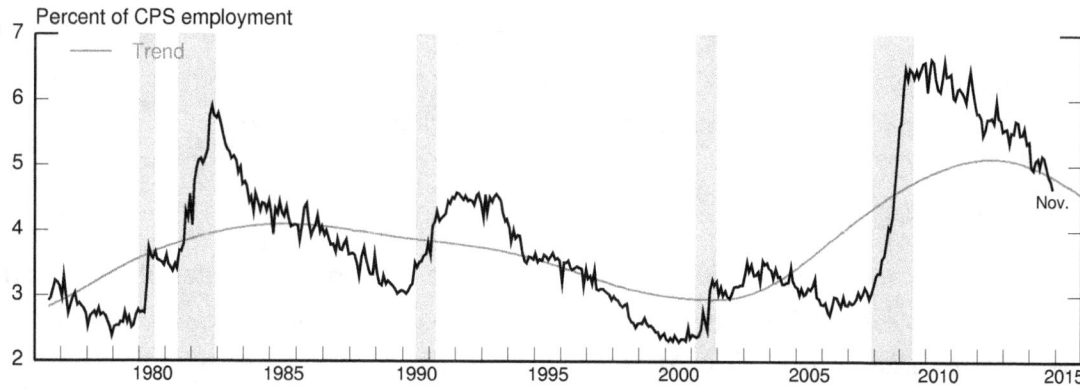

Source: Current Population Survey.
Note: Level up to 1994 adjusted by staff to account for survey redesign. Gray shaded bands indicate a period of business recession as defined by the NBER.

CPS, to measure employment, because it is drawn from a larger survey than the CPS and is less noisy at monthly frequency. We divide total nonfarm employment into *private employment* and *government employment* (Figures 2a and 2b). To render these series stationary, we divide by the civilian noninstitutional population.

We also include *temporary help services employment* (Figure 2c). Temporary help employment may lead overall employment, as firms considering raising payrolls may first hire workers on a temporary basis through a staffing agency. The use of temporary help employment increased noticeably through the mid-1990s, when it reached a relatively stable level about which it has fluctuated since.

2.3 Workweeks

In addition to the number of persons at work, which represents the extensive margin of labor utilization, we included average weekly hours of persons at work to represent an intensive margin. We include two measures of workweeks, taken from different surveys and capturing slightly different concepts. *Average weekly hours of production and nonsupervisory workers* comes from the CES, and measures paid hours per job. We also include a measure of *average weekly hours of persons at work* from respondents in the CPS. As shown in Figures 3a and 3b, both measures increase during expansions and decline during recessions. The CES measure of hours per job appears to have a secular downward trend, whereas the CPS measure of hours per person has fluctuated around 39 hours for most of the sample period.

2.4 Wage Growth

According to most theories, wage inflation is an important indicator of labor market conditions. Aggregate wages are thought to increase faster when conditions in labor markets are tight, because firms must raise wages to attract and retain workers. We include the twelve-month change in (nominal) *average hourly earnings of production and nonsupervisory workers* from the CES (Figure 4). This series is the longest monthly time-series on wages available. Although the BLS's measure of average hourly earnings of all employees is more comprehensive, that series began only in 2005 and so is too short to be usefully included in the model.

2.5 Vacancies

The number of vacant positions at U.S. firms is another important indicator of labor market conditions. Businesses wishing to expand employment typically identify vacant positions, hence the stock of vacancies may proxy for unmet labor demand. For this reason, vacancies play a major role in the large literature on labor-market search and matching.

Figure 2. Employment Indicators

(a) Private Payroll Employment

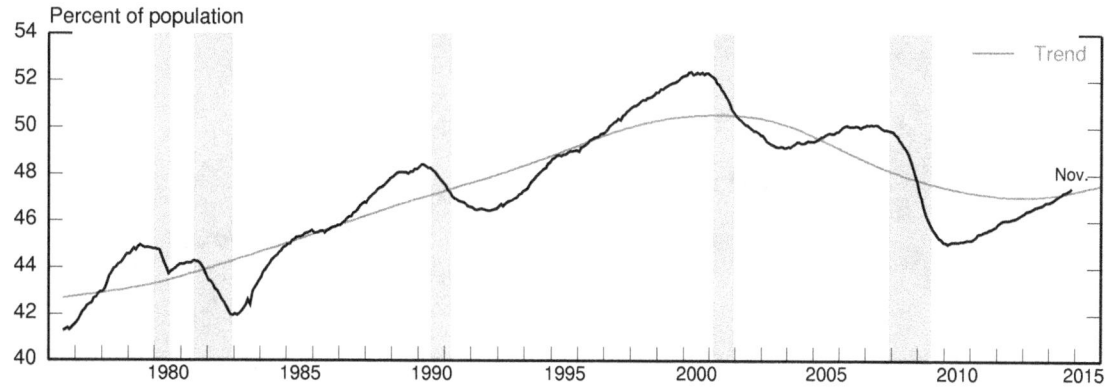

Source: Current Employment Statistics and Current Population Survey.
Note: Gray shaded bands indicate a period of business recession as defined by the NBER.

(b) Government Payroll Employment

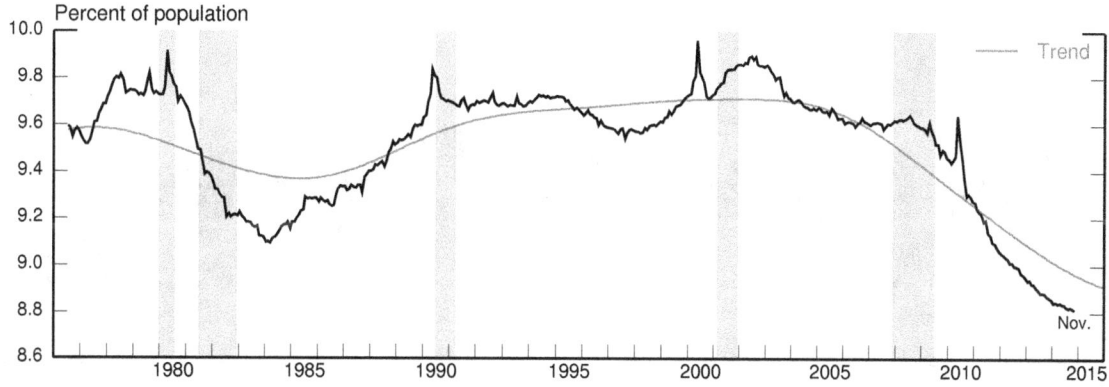

Source: Current Employment Statistics and Current Population Survey.
Note: Gray shaded bands indicate a period of business recession as defined by the NBER.

(c) Temporary Help Employment

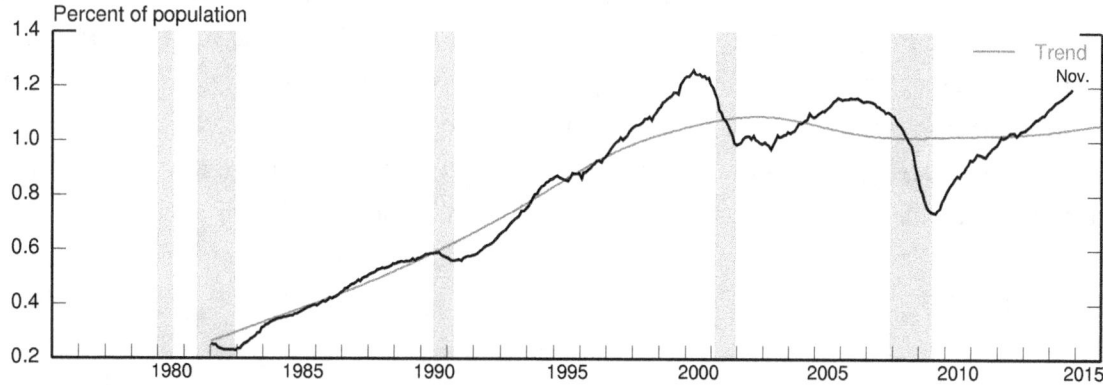

Source: Current Employment Statistics and Current Population Survey.
Note: Gray shaded bands indicate a period of business recession as defined by the NBER.

Figure 3. Workweek Indicators

(a) Average Weekly Hours of Production Workers

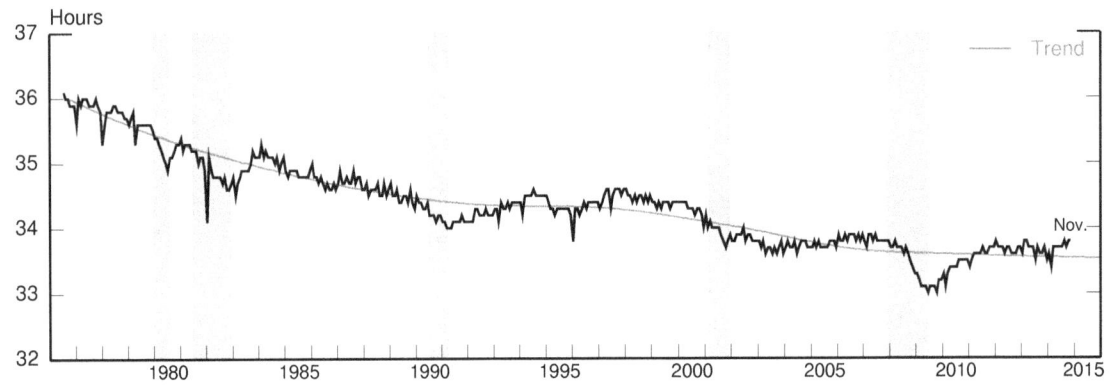

Source: Current Employment Statistics.
Note: Gray shaded bands indicate a period of business recession as defined by the NBER.

(b) Average Weekly Hours of Persons at Work

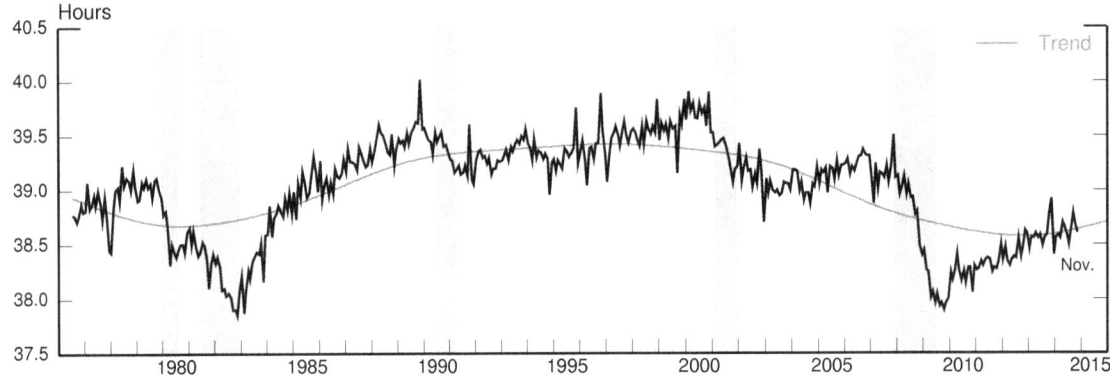

Source: Current Population Survey.
Note: Gray shaded bands indicate a period of business recession as defined by the NBER.

The JOLTS provides a direct measure of vacancies at firms in the scope of the CES. However, this series begins only in December 2000. Moreover, the interaction of the short history of this series and the lag with which the data are published (resulting in a missing contemporaneous value) produced unstable results when we attempted to enter it into the model. For practical reasons, then, we have not included the JOLTS vacancy rate. Instead, we rely on a measure derived from data on help-wanted advertising from the Conference Board as a proxy for vacancies. In particular, we calculate a *composite help-wanted index* following Barnichon (2010) (Figure 5).

Figure 4. Average Hourly Earnings of Production and Nonsupervisory Workers

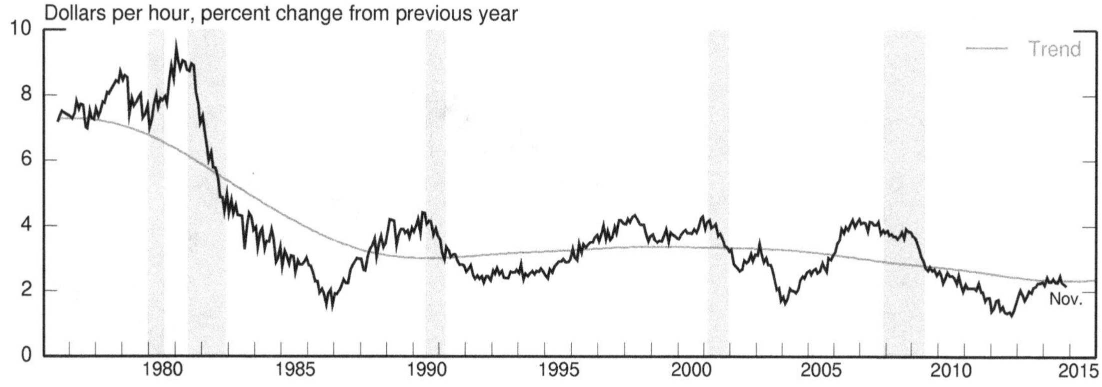

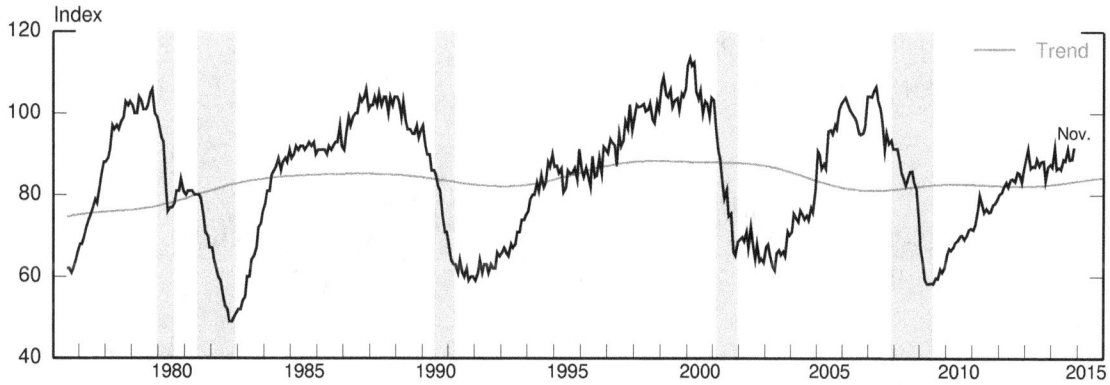

Source: Current Employment Statistics.
Note: Gray shaded bands indicate a period of business recession as defined by the NBER.

Figure 5. Composite Help-Wanted Index

Source: Conference Board and authors' calculations based on Barnichon (2010).
Note: Gray shaded bands indicate a period of business recession as defined by the NBER.

2.6 Hiring

The change in employment can be divided into its component flows of hiring and types of separations. Because these components have different cyclical properties, and can be measured in various ways from various sources, we include measures of the most important (for this purpose) of them in the model.

We include two measures of hiring. The first is the total hiring rate from the JOLTS. Although, as noted above, the JOLTS data begin only in December 2000, Davis, Faberman and Haltiwanger (2012) used gross job creation and destruction rates and their cross-sectional relationship with gross hiring to construct a historical series of hiring rates beginning in 1990:Q2; we use their historical series as data.[4]

---

4. See the appendix for additional details.

Figure 6. Hiring Indicators

(a) Hiring Rate

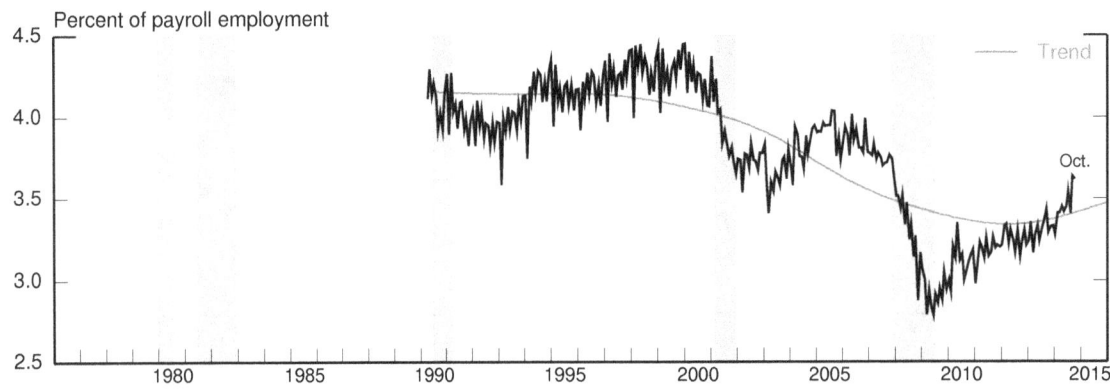

Source: Job Openings and Labor Turnover Survey, Current Employment Statistics, and authors' calculations.
Note: Data before December 2000 were provided by Davis, Faberman and Haltiwanger (2012), who use unpublished microdata to infer series back to 1990:Q2. Gray shaded bands indicate a period of business recession as defined by the NBER.

(b) Transition Rate from Unemployment to Employment

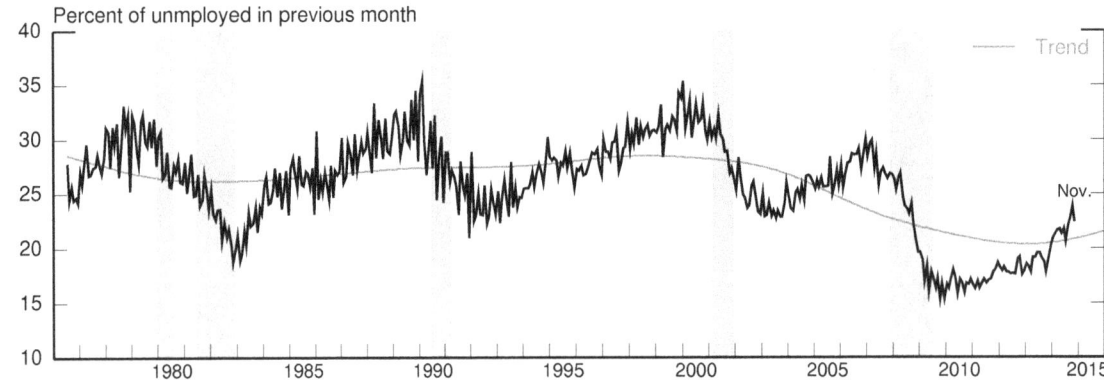

Source: Current Population Survey and authors' calculations.
Note: Gray shaded bands indicate a period of business recession as defined by the NBER.

The second measure of hiring is the transition rate from unemployment to employment calculated from the CPS. Although the latter series measures only a portion of total hiring, it represents a portion that is particularly cyclically sensitive.[5]

2.7   Layoffs

In some respects, unemployment due to layoff may be more reflective of labor demand than is aggregate unemployment, which also includes, for example, that due to labor market entry. We include the *insured unemployment rate* from the Department of Labor's Employment and Train-

---

5. Elsby, Hobijn and Şahin (2013) show that transitions between unemployment and employment account for at least 60 percent of the variation in the unemployment rate.

10

Figure 7. Layoff Indicators

(a) Insured Unemployment Rate

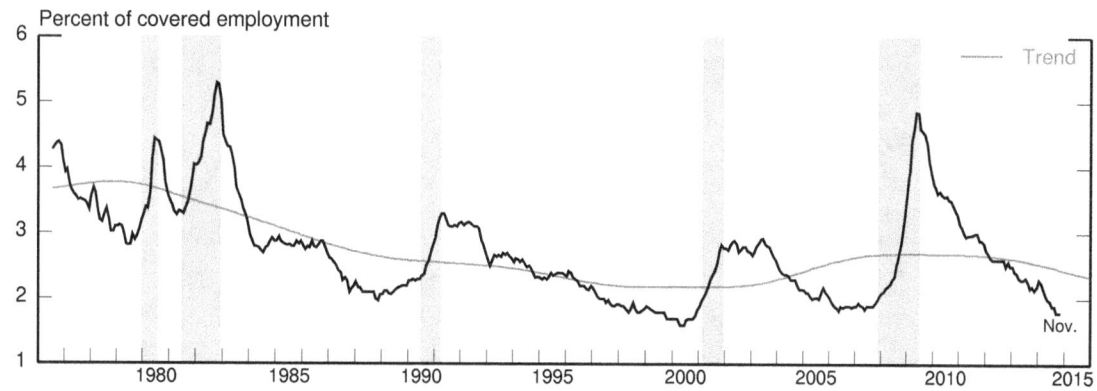

Source: Employment and Training Administration and authors' calculations.
Note: Rate up to 1978 adjusted by staff to account for expansion of UI coverage to include state and local government and nonprofit jobs. Gray shaded bands indicate a period of business recession as defined by the NBER.

(b) Job Losers Unemployed Less than Five Weeks

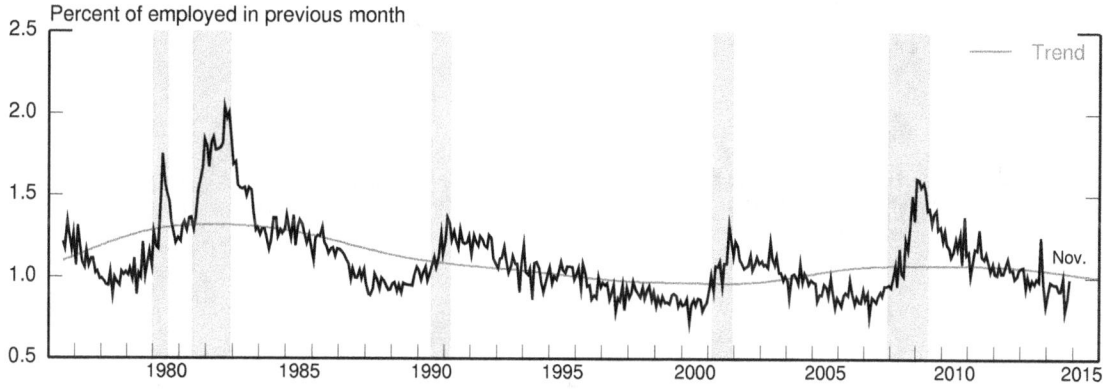

Source: Current Population Survey, seasonally adjusted by authors.
Note: Gray shaded bands indicate a period of business recession as defined by the NBER.

ing Administration as a gauge of the extent of the stock of unemployment due to layoffs, and *job losers unemployed less than five weeks* from the CPS as a measure of the flow into unemployment following layoffs.

2.8 Quits

Separations due to workers quitting behave differently than do separations due to layoffs or other causes. Notably, workers' decisions whether to quit appear to be especially sensitive to their prospects for finding another job. We include two measures of quit rates. The first is the *quit rate* from the JOLTS. As with the hiring rate, we extended this series back to early 1990 using estimates from Davis, Faberman and Haltiwanger (2012). The second is *job leavers*

Figure 8. Quits Indicators

(a) Quit Rate

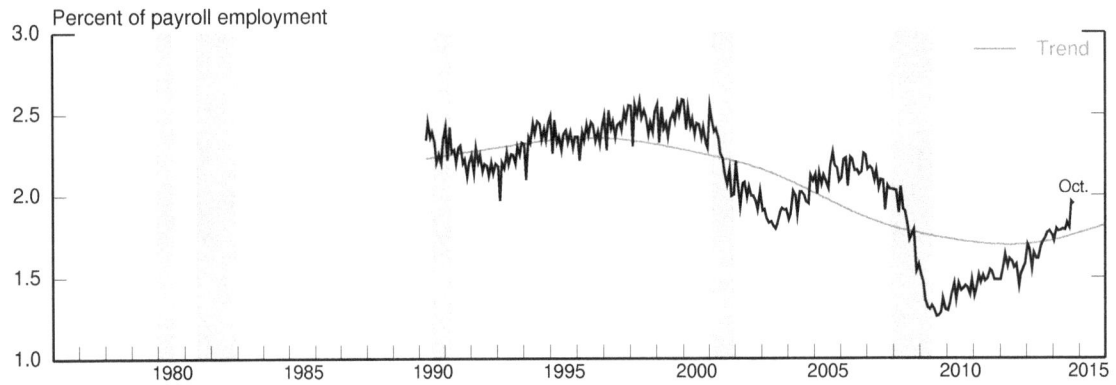

Source: Job Openings and Labor Turnover Survey, Current Employment Statistics, and authors' calculations.
Note: Data before December 2000 were provided by Davis, Faberman and Haltiwanger (2012), who use unpublished microdata to infer series back to 1990:Q2. Gray shaded bands indicate a period of business recession as defined by the NBER.

(b) Job Leavers Unemployed Less than Five Weeks

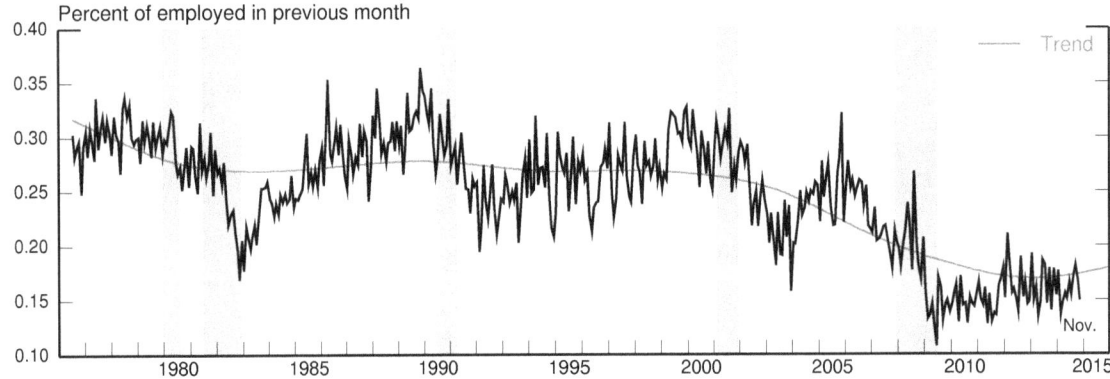

Source: Current Population Survey, seasonally adjusted by authors.
Note: Gray shaded bands indicate a period of business recession as defined by the NBER.

unemployed less than five weeks from the CPS.

2.9 Surveys of Consumers' and Businesses' Perceptions

We include indicators from two private surveys of households and businesses: the Conference Board's Consumer Confidence Survey and the NFIB's Small Business Economic Trends. From the Conference Board, we include a measure of *job availability*, the percent of respondents answering that jobs are plentiful minus the percent answering that jobs are hard to get. From the NFIB we include a measure of small firms' *net hiring plans*, the percent of firms planning to expand employment in the next three months minus percent of firms planning to decrease employment, and one of *unfilled job openings*, the percent of firms with a job opening that they

12

could not fill.

3 A Model of Overall Labor Market Conditions

3.1 The Overall Condition of the Labor Market as a Common Factor

We are interested in constructing an index representing general labor market conditions, in the sense that this index should capture, to as great a degree as possible, common movements in our panel of labor market indicators. One approach to this objective would be to construct the first principal component of the indicators, as in some of the papers noted in the introduction. However, as noted above, our panel of indicators is unbalanced, featuring a number of indicators with relatively short samples. Moreover, we wish to be able to produce stable index estimates contemporaneous with the monthly Employment Situation report, at which time the full panel is not available at the end of the sample. Although methods for estimating principal components with missing data do exist (such as Stock and Watson, 1998), their application to our set of indicators proved unsatisfactory at producing stable estimates of the index; in particular, the resulting estimates revised considerably upon receipt of new observations for the indicators that were missing for the last month of the sample.

In this paper, therefore, we instead estimate a dynamic factor model, along the lines laid out by Geweke (1977) and Sargent and Sims (1977). In a dynamic factor model, as in the principal components framework, the observable vector, Y_t, is a linear combination of a small number of "common" factors, F_t, and an "idiosyncratic" component, ω_t: $Y_t = HF_t + \omega_t$. In turn, the law of motion for the common factors is assumed follow a vector autoregression (VAR). In our case, the persistence implied by the VAR dynamics substantially ameliorates the instability of factor estimates with missing end-of-sample data. As shown by Stock and Watson (1998), as the number of indicators in the panel grows large, principal component and factor analysis are equivalent.

Given our objective of capturing overall labor market conditions, we wish to focus on the common variation which accounts for the largest share of the variance of the indicators. Accordingly, we construct the LMCI as the first principal component of the projection of the indicators onto the common factors.[6] Specifically, let θ be the eigenvector of $H \, var\,(F)\,H^{'}$ associated with the largest eigenvalue. Then

(1) $$\mathrm{LMCI}_t = \theta H F_t.$$

---

6. Of course, the common factors themselves are identified only up to an invertible linear transformation; that is, for any invertible matrix P and set of factor estimates F, there is an observationally equivalent model that yields factor estimates PF.

Figure 9. Surveys of Consumers' and Businesses' Attitudes

(a) Jobs Availability

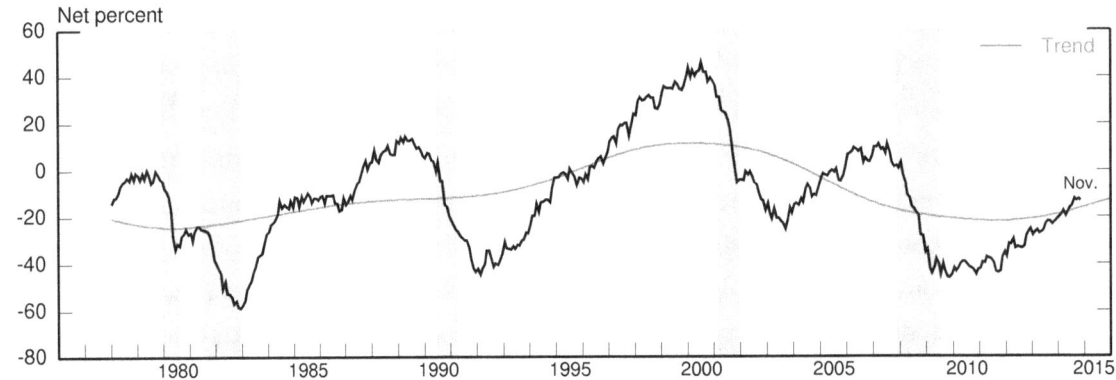

Source: Conference Board

Note: Percent of respondents answering that jobs are plentiful minus percent answering that jobs are hard to get. Gray shaded bands indicate a period of business recession as defined by the NBER.

(b) Net Hiring Plans

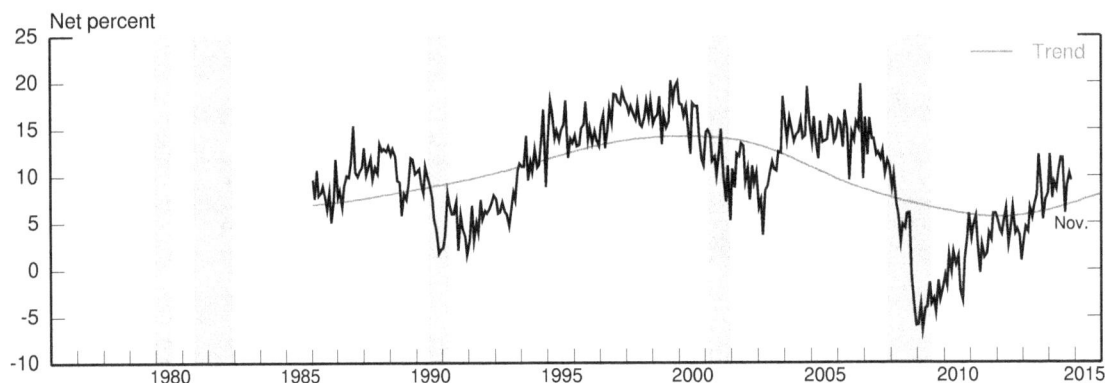

Source: National Federation of Independent Businesses, seasonally adjusted by authors.

Note: Percent of firms planning to expand employment in the next three months minus percent of firms planning to decrease employment. Gray shaded bands indicate a period of business recession as defined by the NBER.

(c) Unfilled Job Openings

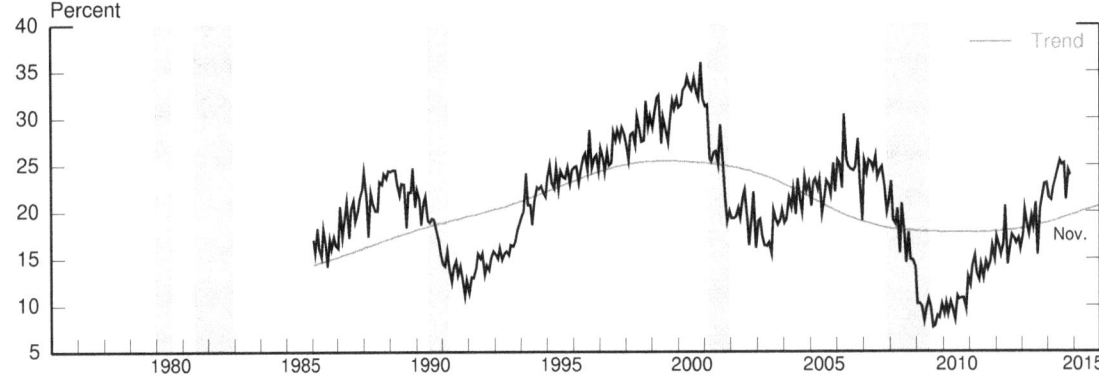

Source: National Federation of Independent Businesses, seasonally adjusted by authors.

Note: Percent of firms with at least one job opening that they could not fill. Gray shaded bands indicate a period of business recession as defined by the NBER.

14

3.2 Detrending

Many of the indicators in our panel appear to display trending behavior and explicit modeling of those low-frequency movements would substantially complicate estimation of the dynamic factor model, while likely contributing little to our primary goal of assessing the cyclical behavior of the labor market. For this reason, before estimating the factor model we detrend each series, using a locally weighted scatterplot smoother (LOWESS) filter with a bandwidth of 16 years (96 months on each side of a data point).[7] This window is about twice as wide as would typically be used for monthly data; however the trends in many of the indicators appear to be lower-frequency than the standard bandwidth, presumably reflecting demographic changes and other slow-moving phenomena. Additionally, this longer bandwidth implies a less volatile trend and, in particular, one that is not heavily influenced by a few months of additional data. As discussed later in section 4, having slow-moving trends makes it easier for us to interpret the change in the LMCI as a signal about aggregate labor market conditions.

Unfortunately, our method for estimating trends is not immune to the endpoint problems associated with other time-series filters. In particular, at the first observation the window is entirely forward-looking, and at the last observation the window is entirely backward-looking.

In order to lessen this problem at the end of the sample, we extend the series forward with simulated data for the purpose of estimating the trend. The simulated data are generated from an autoregressive moving-average (ARMA) equation for each indicator.[8] For most series, beginning-point issues are not a problem, as their history is sufficiently long that the LOWESS trend is fully two-sided by July 1976. However, where the observed history is too short, we simulated 8 years of data backward from the start of the series using its historical relationship with a similar labor market indicator (described in the appendix). These simulated data, both backward and forward, were used only for estimating the level of the trend at the beginning and end of published history; they do not enter the model directly.

Figure 10 provides an illustration of this procedure using the unemployment rate. The black line plots the actual data through November 2014. The model parameters were estimated using data from July 1976 to September 2014, denoted by the unshaded area; the shaded areas show 8 years before and after the estimation sample.[9] The dashed red line is a LOWESS trend based on data only from the estimation sample. The endpoint issues are clear. The blue line is a simulation of the unemployment rate from an ARMA(3,1) model estimated over April 1987 to

---

7. Cleveland (1979). This filter fits a polynomial on a neighborhood of q observations around the estimated point by weighted least squares. We chose the bandwidth for each indicator such that $q = 192$ months.

8. We chose the number of AR terms, the number of MA terms, and whether to include a time trend on a case-by-case basis. These are described in the appendix.

9. Although most indicators were available through November as of this writing, the JOLTS data were only available through October. Therefore, the most recent quarter with data for all indicators was the third quarter, and we chose to end estimation at that point.

Figure 10. Unemployment Rate and Estimated Trends

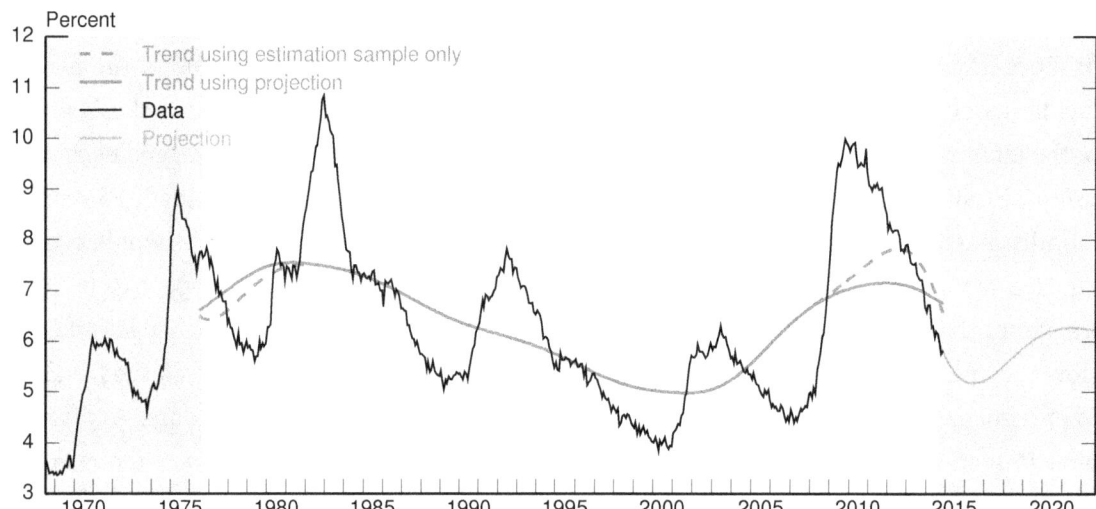

September 2014. The trend we used for the factor model (the solid red line) is computed from a hybrid series that includes the additional 8 years of history plus the 8 years of simulated future data. Although the ARMA equation projections may not prove to be particularly good forecasts, this procedure clearly reduces the endpoint bias.

3.3   The Stationary Dynamic Factor Model

After detrending, observables are related to the common factors via the observation equation

$$(2) \qquad\qquad Y_t = H F_t + \omega_t,$$

where Y_t is a 19×1 vector of labor market indicators, H is a 19×3 matrix of coefficients that map from the three common factors to the indicators, F_t is a 3×1 vector of the common factors. Elements of the idiosyncratic error vector ω_t are assumed to be Gaussian and uncorrelated both across observables and over time. The factors follow a VAR(2) system:

$$(3) \qquad\qquad F_t = A_1 F_{t-1} + A_2 F_{t-2} + \epsilon_t,$$

where ϵ_t is a 3×1 vector of independent and identically distributed Gaussian innovations. The system is estimated by maximizing the likelihood function, computed using the Kalman filter. The ending date for estimation of the trends and model parameters is the final month of the most recent quarter for which all series are available (September 2014 for the analysis in this paper). This date rolls forward every quarter.

The model's 3 factors explain roughly 75 percent of the common variation among the 19

Figure 11. The LMCI

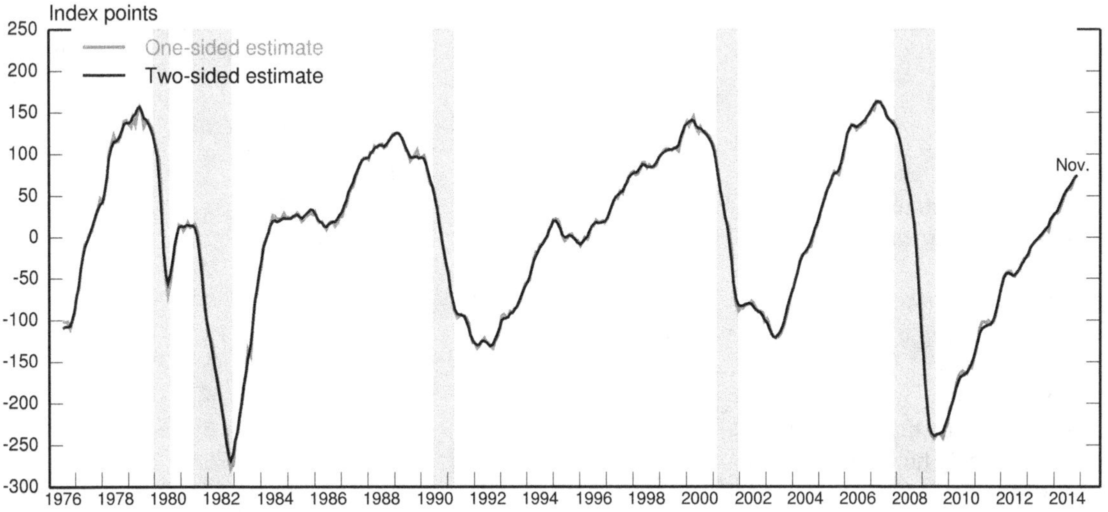

Note: Gray shaded bands indicate a period of business recession as defined by the NBER.

indicators; of this common variation, the LMCI alone accounts for about 85 percent (or 2/3 of the total variation of the indicators).

Figure 11 plots the one- and two-sided estimates of the LMCI obtained using the Kalman smoother algorithm. For the remainder of the paper, we use the two-sided estimate because it provides the best assessment of the labor market conditions given all available information. In practice, and as is visually evident in Figure 11, the one- and two-sided estimates track each other closely over all history.

3.4   Relations between Individual Indicators and the LMCI

Table 2 presents some statistics that describe the relations between individual indicators and the LMCI. The first set of columns reports the Kalman gain on each indicator, a measure of how the current estimate of the LMCI responds to news about a given observable. Because an upward surprise in some indicators would cause the LMCI to revise down (as for the unemployment rate for example) the indicators are ordered in the table by the absolute value of the Kalman gain.[10] Private payroll employment stands out as having a particularly large gain, followed by the two unemployment rates and job availability from the Conference Board survey.

The second set of columns reports the in-sample correlation of the level of the (detrended) indicator with the LMCI. Variables with large gain coefficients tend also to be strongly correlated

---

10. For a few indicators, such as government employment and labor force participation, the gain has a counterintuitive sign. The gains for these indicators are small and probably reflect a heavier loading on common components orthogonal to the LMCI than on the LMCI itself. Such indicators would essentially serve to control for the influence of those orthogonal components.

Table 2. Relations between Individual Indicators and the LMCI

Indicator	Kalman gain		Correlation with LMCI		Correlation with Δ LMCI	
	Value	Rank	Value	Rank	Value	Rank
Private employment	3.44	1	0.92	7	0.83	1
Unemployment rate	−1.91	2	−0.97	1	−0.64	4
Insured unemployment rate	−1.88	3	−0.94	3	−0.74	2
Job availability	1.40	4	0.94	2	0.53	5
Composite help-wanted index	1.37	5	0.93	4	0.47	6
Job losers unemployed less than 5 weeks	−1.03	6	−0.83	13	−0.28	8
Jobs hard to fill	0.96	7	0.93	6	0.20	10
Net hiring plans	0.89	8	0.78	14	0.15	13
Involuntary part-time employment	−0.74	9	−0.93	5	−0.39	7
Average weekly hours of production workers	0.71	10	0.68	15	0.20	9
Hiring rate	0.70	11	0.84	12	0.13	15
Quit rate	0.60	12	0.90	8	0.17	12
Temporary help services employment	0.58	13	0.86	10	0.70	3
Average weekly hours of persons at work	0.50	14	0.85	11	0.17	11
Transition rate from unemployment to employment	0.34	15	0.87	9	0.12	16
Government employment	−0.33	16	0.08	19	−0.03	19
Average hourly earnings of production workers	−0.28	17	0.36	18	0.14	14
Labor force participation rate	−0.24	18	0.52	17	0.06	18
Job leavers unemployed less than 5 weeks	0.11	19	0.63	16	0.06	17

Notes: Indicators are ordered by absolute value of Kalman gain. Kalman gain measures the impact on the current LMCI estimate of a one-standard-deviation forecast error in a given indicator. Correlations are calculated in sample.

with the LMCI, with 7 of the 9 indicators in the top half of the ranking by Kalman gain having correlations in excess of 0.9. By contrast, outside of those 9 indicators, only the quit rate has such a high correlation with the LMCI. The final two columns report the correlation of the over-the-month change in each indicator with the change in the LMCI. The ranking by correlation in changes is also similar to the ranking by the gains. Notably, however, whereas in levels the unemployment rate was the most highly correlated with the LMCI, in changes that distinction belongs to private employment.

While all of these measures identify broadly the same set of variables as especially influential, the detailed rankings may differ, for two noteworthy reasons. First, the Kalman gain is a multivariate concept, analogous to a partial derivative, that takes into account the contributions of other indicators. The gain for a given indicator is therefore sensitive to the assumed presence of the full set of other indicators. Were this information set to change, the gains would also be different. The correlations, in contrast, are more analogous to total derivatives: The correlation between a given indicator and the LMCI can reflect contributions to the index of other indicators that are correlated with the given indicator.

18

Second, the Kalman gain refers to the influence of a single month's news about an indicator on the current month's value of the index. However, the full contribution of an indicator to the index is also affected by the degree to which the effects of the news are propagated forward and backward in time, a property essentially controlled by the VAR dynamics in equation 3. These differences explain why, for example, the unemployment rate can have the highest pairwise correlation with the LMCI but a much lower gain than private employment.

We found two results from this exercise surprising. The first is the strong signal the model takes from the indicators of consumers' and businesses' perceptions of labor market conditions, most notably that of job availability. Our prior was that "subjective" indicators like these would have little additional contribution after including hard data such as the unemployment rate, hiring, and vacancies. The second is the relatively weak signal the model takes from the indicators of quits, as we think of quits as strongly related to labor market conditions. It is possible that the relatively low gain on the indicators of quits reflect a combination of monthly noise in the CPS measure of job leavers and the short history of the JOLTS quit rate.

4   Levels versus Changes

Figure 11 shows the level of the LMCI. Not surprisingly, its peaks and troughs align fairly closely with business cycles identified by the National Bureau of Economic Research (NBER). However, in our view, the level of the index itself, and notably an LMCI equal to zero, has no obvious economically meaningful interpretation. In particular, the level of the index itself is severely limited as a gauge of the labor market slack, or the distance of the labor market from full employment. This is so for three reasons.

First, by construction the index has an expected value of zero over the period of estimation. However, it is far from clear that the economy is at full employment on average over that particular period, or over any long period. We have not attempted to estimate a level for the LMCI that would correspond to, for example, the natural rate of unemployment.

Second, the trends in the indicators that enter the estimation of the index were not designed to be informative about the full-employment levels of each series. This is particularly important if, as is likely, the full-employment levels of those series have evolved over time. For this reason comparisons of the level of the LMCI over long periods are not by themselves reliable. Moreover, as good as a LOWESS procedure is, the estimated trends may be influenced by the business cycle, and, despite the ARMA augmentation, may be subject to endpoint bias from such a major long period of weakness as the U.S. labor market has experienced in the present cycle. Third, and related to the above, the index captures common movements only among the cyclical deviations of the indicators from their estimated trends, neglecting any common movements in those trends.

A few examples highlight our concern. As shown in Figure 1a, the unemployment rate has been below the estimated trend since the end of 2013. We believe this is because the LOWESS-generated trend for the unemployment rate has been pulled up by the deep recession and slow recovery. In a similar vein, we believe the trends for part-time for economic reasons (Figure 1c) and private payroll employment to be above and below, respectively, levels consistent with full employment.[11] As suggested by the figures, these biases are probably in play for the estimates of trend even before the recession, with the result that the LMCI reaches its highest level in 2007. We find it implausible that the labor market was tighter in 2007 than it was in, say, 2000.

However, because the common components of the trends are slow moving in our specification, we believe that short-run changes in the index are informative about movements in overall labor market conditions. For that reason in the remainder of the paper we will concentrate on changes in, rather than levels of the LMCI, and changes at a reasonably high frequency.

5   Changes in Labor Market Conditions through the Lens of the LMCI

Figure 12 plots the average monthly change in the LMCI since the second half of 1976. Except for the final bar, which extends only through November 2014, each of the bars represents the average over a six-month period.

Not surprisingly, changes in the LMCI align well with business cycles as defined by the NBER. That is, the LMCI generally declines during recessions (the grey shaded areas) and typically rises during expansions. And the magnitudes of the declines accord with most observers' assessments of the severity of those recessions. The average monthly increase in the LMCI so far during the current expansion has been roughly in line with previous expansions, but, of course, follows much larger average monthly declines during the preceding recession.

5.1   Decomposing the LMCI into Contributions of Individual Indicators

We can gain more insight into the determinants of the LMCI estimates by explicitly computing the dependence of the estimated LMCI path on the data for each indicator. Specifically, given the linear-Gaussian specification for our dynamic factor model, the paths of the LMCI and the indicators have a joint multivariate normal distribution. As a general property of such distributions, the expected path of the LMCI, conditional on the data, is linear in the indicators. Thus, we can decompose the estimated LMCI path into contributions from each indicator, holding the remaining indicators constant. As the estimate is two-sided, in principle the entire history

---

11. Using the series without detrending would create its own set of problems, as it would implicitly assume that the trend in each series was constant at the mean of the series.

Figure 12. Average Monthly Change in LMCI

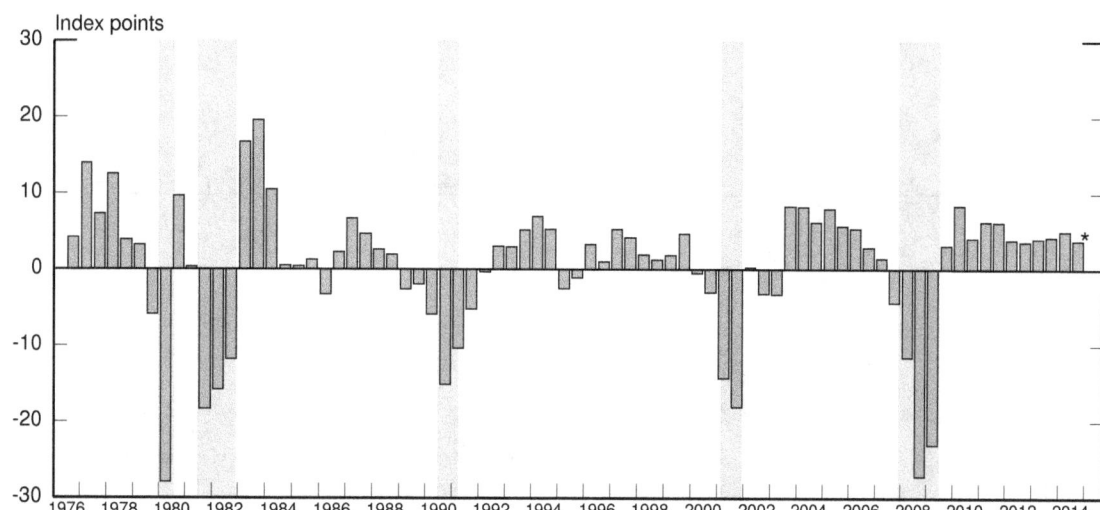

Note: Each bar is the average monthly change over a six-month period. Gray shaded bands indicate a period of business recession as defined by the NBER. * The bar for 2014:H2 is the average monthly change for July through November.

of each indicator's deviation from its trend influences the estimated LMCI at any given date.[12] However, in practice, the estimated LMCI for a particular date depends to any significant degree only on observations in a narrow window around that date. In particular, only the last six months receive any substantial weight in determining the estimated LMCI at the end of the sample.

The calculation of these contributions is easily done using the standard Kalman filter and smoothing recursions. Let us write $Z_t = [F_t; F_{t-1}]$ and $W = [A_1, A_2]$. Then the standard Kalman filter recursion can be expressed in the form

$$(4) \qquad Z_{t|t} = (1 - B) W Z_{t-1|t-1} + BY_t$$

$$(5) \qquad = \sum_{s=t_0}^{t} [(1 - B) W]^{s-t_0} BY_s$$

where B is the Kalman gain matrix. The corresponding decomposition of the two-sided estimates is straightforward.

---

12. This represents a stark deviation from a principal components model in which the current level of the principal component is a weighted average of the current indicators only. We believe the richer structure of our model's decomposition, while complex, is desirable.

21

Figure 13. Change in LMCI and its Decomposition since 2007

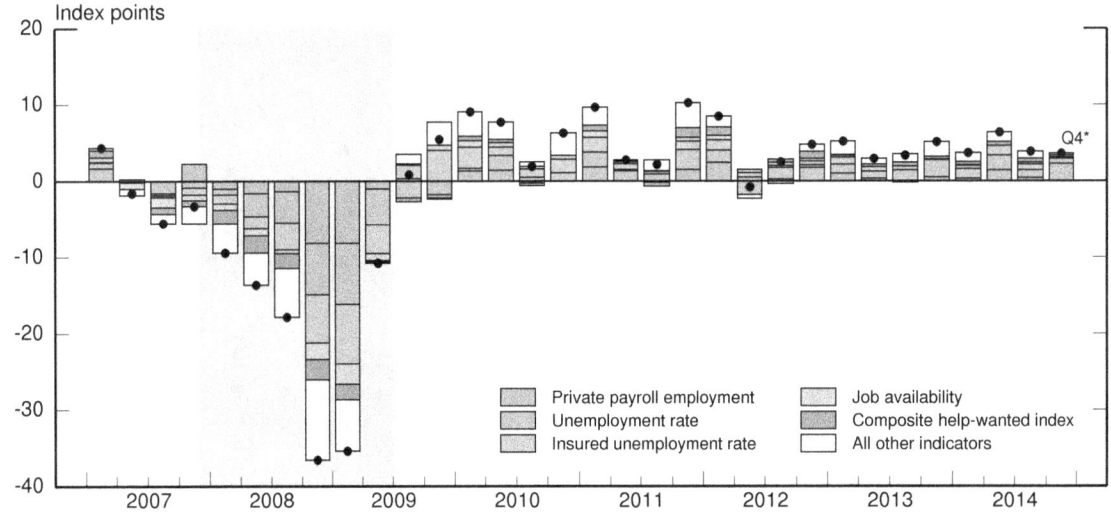

Notes: The solid black circle is the average monthly change in each quarter; the stacked bars are the contribution of an indicator to the average monthly change. Gray shaded band indicates a period of business recession as defined by the NBER. * Average monthly change for 2014:Q4 is the average of October and November.

5.2 Changes in Labor Market Conditions since 2007

Figure 13 zooms in on the Great Recession and ongoing recovery. The solid black circles mark the average monthly change in the LMCI in each quarter since 2007. The LMCI began falling in the second quarter of 2007 and deteriorated sharply in late 2008 and early 2009, as the financial crisis reached its height. The LMCI started improving in the second half of 2009. The uneven pace of the ongoing labor market recovery is apparent at this time scale. Indeed, the LMCI captures several periods of sluggish improvement in the early parts of 2010, 2011, and 2012. The particularly marked, but temporary, slowdown in labor market improvement in the second quarter of 2012 stands out.

The stacked bars decompose the total changes into the contributions of the five most influential indicators, plus the sum of the contributions of all other indicators. Over the recovery, as is typical, a few indicators have accounted for the bulk of the increase in the LMCI. In the first two years of the recovery, the insured unemployment rate (the green portion of the bars) made a large contribution to the improvement in the LMCI, reflecting a substantial slowing in layoffs; this contribution has since diminished. Gains in private payroll employment (the blue portion of the bars) and declines in the unemployment rate (the pink portion of the bars) have been consistent contributors to the improvement, although more in some years than in others. In 2014, private employment and the unemployment rate have accounted for most of the improvement in the LMCI.

6   Has the Unemployment Rate Overstated Recent Improvements in Labor Market Conditions?

The unemployment rate has declined by 2 percentage points since the end of 2012. This brisk pace of decline, set against the backdrop of a more modest improvement in real GDP and other indicators, led some to wonder whether the unemployment rate has overstated the improvement in labor market conditions. For example, in the press conference after the September 2014 Federal Open Market Committee meeting, Federal Reserve Chair Janet Yellen pointed to two factors suggesting less improvement: the decline in labor force participation and elevated share of involuntary part-time employment.[13] Our model provides a direct and transparent way to assess this and other questions arising when the model's indicators appear to send different signals about labor market conditions. This section examines whether the unemployment rate has been sending a more positive signal than have the other indicators.

To see how one can use a dynamic factor model to analyze movements in one of the indicators vis-à-vis the other indicators, recall equation 2, which relates the unobserved factors to the indicators. From that relationship, one can generate a prediction for the indicators by generating a "fitted" value from the estimated coefficients and estimated factors. The left panel of Figure 14 shows this model prediction for the unemployment rate since 2005. It is no surprise that the predicted unemployment rate tracks the actual unemployment rate quite closely—we showed in section 3.4 that the LMCI and the unemployment rate are highly correlated. Note that this predicted value in effect "controls for" the behavior of the other indicators, notably the LFPR and involuntary part-time employment.

Although the LMCI's prediction for the unemployment rate generally tracks the actual unemployment rate closely, there are periods when the two differ. Looking over the past few years, between 2011 and 2012, the unemployment rate was higher than the model's prediction based on its indicators, but over the latter half of 2013 and through 2014 the actual unemployment rate fell below the model's prediction. Although the unemployment rate in November stood only about 0.1 percentage point below the model's prediction, the unemployment rate has declined by about 1/4 percentage point more than the LMCI's predicted value since the end of 2012.

Given these discrepancies, the question arises: What would the change in labor market conditions have looked like had the model not seen the decline in the unemployment rate? Again, the structure of the LMCI offers a natural way to conduct this experiment. When missing values for some of the observables (the elements of Y_t), the model generates expectations for all of the indicators based on the assumed dynamics of the factors and their relationship to the indicators. To be precise, given an estimate of the factors in month t (F_t), the model forms an

---

13. http://www.federalreserve.gov/mediacenter/files/FOMCpresconf20140917.pdf, p. 11–12.

Figure 14. Has the Unemployment Rate Overstated the Improvement in Labor Market Conditions?

(a) Unemployment Rate and Model Prediction   (b) Average Monthly Change in LMCI

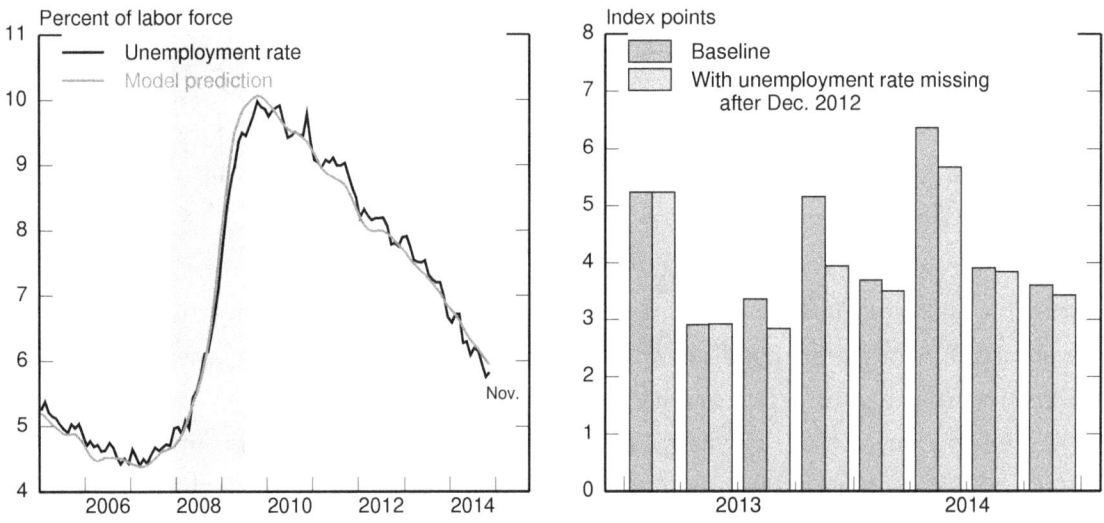

Note: Gray shaded band indicates a period of business recession as defined by the NBER. Average monthly change for 2014:Q4 is the average of October and November.

expectation of the observables in month $T \geq t$ via the following equation:

$$(6) \qquad \mathrm{E}\left[\boldsymbol{Y}_T \mid \{\boldsymbol{Y}_s, s \leq t\}, \{\tilde{\boldsymbol{Y}}_u, t < u \leq T\}\right] = \boldsymbol{H}\mathrm{E}\left[\boldsymbol{F}_T \mid \{\boldsymbol{Y}_s, s \leq t\}, \{\tilde{\boldsymbol{Y}}_u, t < u \leq T\}\right],$$

where $\tilde{Y}$ contains all available indicators after month t *except* the unemployment rate. We estimate a version of the LMCI that deletes observations for the unemployment rate starting in 2013.

The right panel of Figure 14 plots the average monthly change in the LMCI (the blue bars) for each quarter from 2013 forward together with the average monthly change in the LMCI when the unemployment rate was not observed after December 2012 (the orange bars). It is visually apparent from the panel that the the yellow bars are lower than the blue bars from the second half of 2013 through the end of 2014. Although the magnitude is modest—the average monthly change was 0.3 point slower when the model did not observe the unemployment rate than when it did—the constellation of labor market indicators excluding the unemployment rate suggests slightly less improvement in labor market conditions.

7 Closing Remarks

Overall, the LMCI appears to be a useful tool for assessing the change in labor market conditions based on a broad array of labor market indicators. Of course, any purely statistical procedure will be sensitive to the many choices one must make in specifying the model. Moreover, such a procedure will not be able to flexibly discount idiosyncratic events nor to account for changes in economic structures. Such a model is, therefore, no substitute for judicious consideration of the various indicators. Nevertheless, such a model provides a summary that can usefully inform those deliberations.

Not surprisingly, given the nature of business cycles, the LMCI is highly correlated with the unemployment rate, as it is individually with several other prominent labor market indicators. Of course, we could not be sure this would be the case before developing the LMCI, but that done, one may ask whether the LMCI adds to consideration of the unemployment rate alone. We think that it does. Although the LMCI and the unemployment rate may move in reasonably close tandem on average, it is precisely in those times when movements in the unemployment rate seems to be at variance with other indicators that a tool for summarizing a large number of indicators is most valuable. That is, the LMCI is one way to organize discussions of the signal value of a number of different labor market indicators in situations when they might be sending diverse signals.

Examples of such situations are not hard to find, such as recent discussions about whether the unemployment rate has been overstating the degree of improvement in the labor market. Answering this question requires one to compare the unemployment rate with other labor market indicators. The LMCI, and multivariate methods like it, are well-suited for that task. Indeed, from the perspective of the LMCI, the unemployment rate has improved slightly faster than is consistent with the signal from the other indicators over the past two years.

Appendix

Detrending Procedure

In order to mitigate endpoint bias, we project each indicator forward with simulated data. The simulated data are generated from an ARMA equation for each indicator. The specifications are given in Table A1. The estimation period for the projection model is from April 1987 through the last month of the most recent quarter for which all data are available. Starting in 1987 allows us to omit time trends from most equations.

In addition, for some series for which the observed history is short, we also simulated 8 years of data backward from the start of the series, as described below.

Backcasted Series

Temporary help services employment was projected backward (as a percent of population) using private employment (as a percent of population) and a linear time trend. The equation was estimated using data from the first observation in January 1982 through December 1992. We used a this period to infer the historical relationship because temporary help employment rose rapidly as a share of employment in the mid-1990s and then stabilized from about 1997 forward.

Hiring rate and quit rate. Davis, Faberman and Haltiwanger (2012) used unpublished JOLTS microdata to infer quits and hires that extend back to April 1990. We first interpolated the quarterly data from DFH to monthly series covering from April 1990 to November 2000; we appended these to the published data, which begin in Decmeber 2000. We then treat that hybrid series as data in the factor model. To estimate a two-sided trend, we projected the series back 8 years using the transition rates from unemployment to employment (hiring rate) and employment to unemployment (quit rate) computed from the CPS. The backcasting equations were estimated using data from their first observation in April 1990 through June 2005.

Job losers unemployed less than five weeks, job leavers unemployed less than five weeks, net hiring plans, unfilled job openings, and job availability. These five indicators were projected backward using the unemployment rate. The equations were estimated using data from their first observation through June 2005.

Data sources

Underlying source data used to construct the indicators listed in Table 1 are listed in Table A2.

Table A1. Specification for Projection Equations

Indicator	ARMA(p,q) model used to project series		
	AR	MA	Other
Unemployment and underemployment			
Unemployment rate	3	1	
Labor force participation rate	1	1	t^2
Involuntary part-time employment	3	1	
Employment			
Private employment	3	1	
Government employment	1	0	
Temporary help services employment	2	1	
Workweeks			
Average weekly hours of production workers	3	1	t
Average weekly hours of persons at work	3	1	
Wages			
Average hourly earnings of production workers	1	1	
Vacancies			
Composite help-wanted index	3	1	
Hiring			
Hiring rate	1	1	
Transition rate from unemployment to employment	3	1	
Layoffs			
Insured unemployment rate	2	1	
Job losers unemployed less than five weeks	2	1	
Quits			
Quit rate	1	1	
Job leavers unemployed less than five weeks	1	1	
Consumer and business surveys			
Job availability	3	1	
Net hiring plans	2	1	
Unfilled jobs openings	1	1	

Table A2. Underlying Source Data

Series	Source	SA/NSA	Units	BLS retrieval code	FRED series name	First value	Final value
Civilian noninstitutional population[1]	CPS	NSA	Thousands	LNU00000000	CNP16OV	1948m1	n.a.
Labor force level[1]	CPS	SA	Thousands	LNS11000000	CLF16OV	1948m1	n.a.
Employment level[1]	CPS	SA	Thousands	LNS12000000	CE16OV	1948m1	n.a.
Unemployment level[1]	CPS	SA	Thousands	LNS13000000	UNRATE	1948m1	n.a.
Employment level - Part-time for economic reasons, all industries[2]	CPS	SA	Thousands	LNS12032194	LNS12032194	1955m5	n.a.
Employment - Total nonfarm	CES	SA	Thousands	CES0000000001	PAYEMS	1939m1	n.a.
Employment - Total private	CES	SA	Thousands	CES0500000001	USPRIV	1939m1	n.a.
Employment - Government	CES	SA	Thousands	CES9000000001	USGOVT	1939m1	n.a.
Employment - Temporary help services	CES	SA	Thousands	CES6056132001	TEMPHELPS	1990m1	n.a.
Employment - Help supply services[3]	CES	SA	Thousands	n.a.	n.a.	1982m1	2003m4
Average weekly hours of production and nonsupervisory employees - Total private	CES	SA	Hours	CES0500000007	AWHNONAG	1964m1	n.a.
Average weekly hours - Total at work, all industries[4]	CPS	NSA	Hours	LNU02005054	n.a.	1976m6	n.a.

(Continued)

Table A2. Underlying Source Data (continued)

Series	Source	SA/NSA	Units	BLS retrieval code	FRED series name	First value	Final value
Average hourly earnings of production and nonsupervisory employees - Total private	CES	SA	Dollars per hour	CES0500000008	AHETPI	1964m1	n.a.
Hires - Total nonfarm[5]	JOLTS	SA	Thousands	JTS000000000HIL	JTSHIL	1990m4	n.a.
Quits - Total nonfarm[5]	JOLTS	SA	Thousands	JTS000000000QUL	JTSQUL	1990m4	n.a.
Labor force flows - Unemployed to employed[6]	CPS	SA	Thousands	LNS17100000	LNS17100000	1967m7	n.a.
Labor force flows - Employed to unemployed[6]	CPS	SA	Thousands	LNS17400000	LNS17400000	1967m7	n.a.
Insured unemployment rate[7]	ETA	SA	Percent of covered employemnt	n.a.	IURSA	1971m1	n.a.
Percent of total job losers unemployed less than 5 weeks[4]	CPS	NSA	Percent of CPS employment	LNU03023633	n.a.	1976m6	n.a.
Percent of total job leavers unemployed less than 5 weeks[4]	CPS	NSA	Percent of CPS employment	LNU03023717	n.a.	1976m6	n.a.
Unemployment level - Job leavers	CPS	SA	Thousands	LNS13023705	LNS13023705	1967m1	n.a.
Help-wanted advertising index	CB	SA	Index	n.a.	n.a.	1951m1	2010m10
Total online help-wanted ads	CB	SA	Thousands of ads	n.a.	n.a.	2005m5	n.a.
Employment - Jobs plentiful	CB	SA	Percent of individuals surveyed	n.a.	n.a.	1978m1	n.a.

(Continued)

Table A2. Underlying Source Data (continued)

Series	Source	SA/NSA	Units	BLS retrieval code	FRED series name	First value	Final value
Employment - Jobs hard to get	CB	SA	Percent of individuals surveyed	n.a.	n.a.	1978m1	n.a.
Job openings[4]	NFIB	NSA	Percent of firms with a job opening they could not fill	n.a.	n.a.	1986m1	n.a.
Net hiring plans[4]	NFIB	NSA	Percent of firms planning to expand employment in the next 3 months minus percent of firms planning to decrease employment	n.a.	n.a.	1986m1	n.a.

Notes: CB = Conference Board and Barnichon (2010); CES = Bureau of Labor Statistics, Current Employment Statistics; CPS = Bureau of Labor Statistics, Current Population Survey; ETA = Department of Labor, Employment and Training Administration; JOLTS = Bureau of Labor Statistics, Job Openings and Labor Turnover Survey; NFIB = National Federation of Independent Business.

1. Level adjusted by authors to account for changes in population weights.
2. Level up to December 1993 adjusted by authors to account for the CPS redesign. See Polivka and Miller (1998).
3. SIC 7363.
4. Seasonally adjusted by authors.
5. Data before December 2000 were provided by Davis, Faberman and Haltiwanger (2012), who use unpublished JOLTS microdata to infer series back to 1990:Q2.
6. Data before January 1994 are authors' calculations from CPS microdata.
7. Converted to monthly and adjusted before 1978 by authors to account for expansion of UI coverage to include state and local government and nonprofit jobs.

References

Aaronson, Stephanie, Tomaz Cajner, Bruce Fallick, Felix Galbis-Reig, Christopher Smith, and William Wascher. 2014. "Labor Force Participation: Recent Developments and Future Prospects." *Brookings Papers on Economic Activity*, 2.

Barnes, Michelle, Ryan Chahrour, Giovanni Olivei, and Gaoyan Tang. 2007. "A Principal Components Approach to Estimating Labor Market Pressure and Its Implications for Inflation." Federal Reserve Bank of Boston Public Policy Brief 07-2.

Barnichon, Regis. 2010. "Building a Composite Help-Wanted Index." *Economics Letters*, 109(3): 175–78.

Cleveland, William S. 1979. "Robust Locally Weighted Regression and Smoothing Scatterplots." *Journal of the American Statistical Association*, 74(368): 829–36.

Davis, Steven J., R. Jason Faberman, and John Haltiwanger. 2012. "Labor Market Flows in the Cross Section and over Time." *Journal of Monetary Economics*, 59(1): 1–18.

Elsby, Michael W. L., Bart Hobijn, and Ayşegül Şahin. 2013. "On the Importance of the Participation Margin for Market Fluctuations." Federal Reserve Bank of San Francisco Working Paper 2013–05.

Geweke, John. 1977. "The Dynamic Factor Analysis of Economic Time Series." In *Latent Variables in Socio-Economic Models*. , ed. Dennis J. Aigner and Arthur S. Goldberger, Ch. 19. North-Holland Publishing Co.

Giannone, Domenico, Lucrezia Reichlin, and David Small. 2008. "Nowcasting: The Real-Time Informational Content of Macroeconomic Data." *Journal of Monetary Economics*, 55(4): 665–76.

Hakkio, Craig S., and Jonathan L. Willis. 2013. "Assessing Labor Market Conditions: The Level of Activity and the Speed of Improvement." Federal Reserve Bank of Kansas City Macro Bulletin (July 18).

Polivka, Anne E., and Stephen M. Miller. 1998. "The CPS after the Redesign: Refocusing the Economic Lens." In *Labor Statistics Measurement Issues*. 249–89. University of Chicago Press.

Sargent, Thomas J., and Christoper A. Sims. 1977. "Business Cycle Modeling without Pretending to Have Too Much A Priori Economic Theory." In *New Methods in Business Cycle Research*. , ed. Christopher Sims. Federal Reserve Bank of Minneapolis.

Stock, James H., and Mark W. Watson. 1998. "Diffusion Indexes." NBER Working Paper 6702.

Stock, James H., and Mark W. Watson. 2002. "Macroeconomic Forecasting Using Diffusion Indexes." *Journal of Business & Economic Statistics*, 20(2): 147–62.

Stock, James H., and Mark W. Watson. 2011. "Dynamic Factor Models." In *Oxford Handbook of Economic Forecasting*. , ed. Michael P. Clements and David F. Hendry, 35–59. Oxford University Press.

Zmitrowicz, Konrad, and Mikael Khan. 2014. "Beyond the Unemployment Rate: Assessing Canadian and U.S. Labor Markets Since the Great Recession." *Band of Canada Review*, Spring: 42–53.